AF228515

XTREME CARS

PORSCHE

A&D Xtreme
BOLD HI-LO NONFICTION
An imprint of Abdo Publishing
abdobooks.com

S.L. HAMILTON

ABDOBOOKS.COM

Published by Abdo Publishing, a division of ABDO, PO Box 398166, Minneapolis, Minnesota 55439. Copyright © 2023 by Abdo Consulting Group, Inc. International copyrights reserved in all countries. No part of this book may be reproduced in any form without written permission from the publisher. A&D Xtreme™ is a trademark and logo of Abdo Publishing.

052022
092022

Editor: John Hamilton

Copy Editor: Tamara L. Britton

Graphic Design: Sue Hamilton

Cover Design: Laura Graphenteen

Cover Photo: Shutterstock

Interior Photos & Illustrations: All photos Dr. Ing. h.c. F. Porsche AG, except: Alamy-pgs 24-25; Cars and Bids-pg 26; Classic Driver-pg 18-19; Getty/iStock-pgs 10-11, 22-23, 34-35 & 42-43; Larry Barbier Jr-pg 11 (top inset); Shutterstock-pgs 8-9, 12-13, 14-15, 20-21, 27, 30-31 & 32-33.

LIBRARY OF CONGRESS CONTROL NUMBER: 2021942761

PUBLISHER'S CATALOGING-IN-PUBLICATION DATA

Names: Hamilton, S.L., author.

Title: Porsche / by S.L. Hamilton

Description: Minneapolis, Minnesota : Abdo Publishing, 2023 | Series: Xtreme cars | Includes online resources and index.

Identifiers: ISBN 9781532196096 (lib. bdg.) | ISBN 9781098217020 (ebook)

Subjects: LCSH: Porsche automobiles--Juvenile literature. | Sports cars-- Juvenile literature. | Cars (Automobiles)--Juvenile literature.

Classification: DDC 629.2221--dc23

TABLE OF CONTENTS

CHAPTER 1

PORSCHE—THERE IS NO SUBSTITUTE

Porsches are known for their performance and **luxury**. Their speed, classic shape, and beautiful interiors have made them some of the world's most popular sports cars. Many Porsche fans believe there is no substitute.

XTREME FACT

The correct way to pronounce "Porsche" is as a two-syllable word: "Por-shuh."

PORSCHE

718 Cayman

PORSCHE'S HISTORY

Exterior designer Erwin Komenda, Ferry Porsche, and Ferdinand Porsche stand next to the first 356.

Ferdinand "Ferry" Porsche said, "I looked around and could not find quite the car I dreamed of, so I decided to build it myself." The Porsche company was established in 1948 in Gmünd, Austria. The first **production car** was the Porsche 356.

XTREME FACT

Ferdinand Porsche Sr. (Ferry's father) was a race car driver and engineer. He founded his own company in the 1930s and helped develop Germany's Volkswagen Beetle. Parts of the Beetle's design were used in Ferry's Porsche 356.

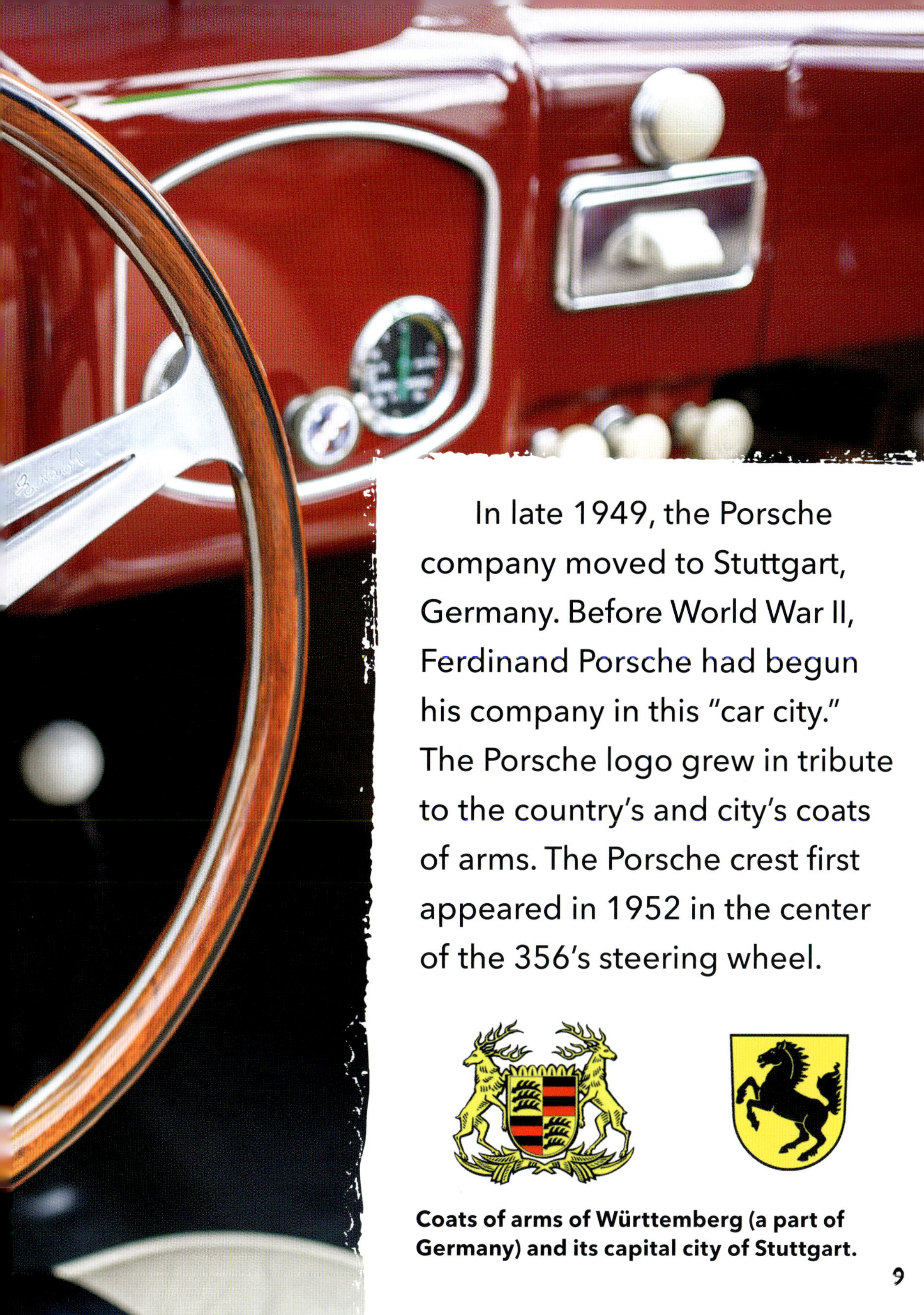

In late 1949, the Porsche company moved to Stuttgart, Germany. Before World War II, Ferdinand Porsche had begun his company in this "car city." The Porsche logo grew in tribute to the country's and city's coats of arms. The Porsche crest first appeared in 1952 in the center of the 356's steering wheel.

Coats of arms of Württemberg (a part of Germany) and its capital city of Stuttgart.

CHAPTER 3

PORSCHE 356

Movie and rock stars made Porsche 356s one of the most-wanted sports cars of the time. The rear-engine, 2-seater was designed with style, speed, and driveability. Over its 17 production years, the 356 had many improvements. This included being made as both a **coupe** and a **cabriolet**.

The 356 Roadster had a top speed of 109 mph (175 kph).

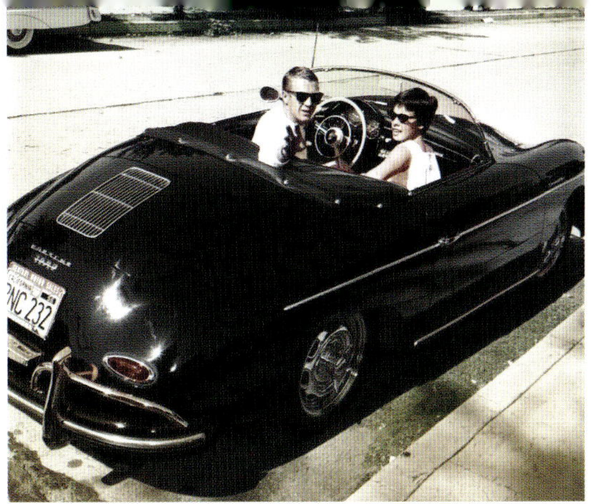

Actor Steve McQueen owned and raced a 1958 Porsche 356 Speedster 1600.

PORSCHE 356 SPECIFICATIONS

YEARS PRODUCED
1948-1965

MAXIMUM HORSEPOWER
75 (1958 Speedster model)

ZERO TO 60 MPH (97 KPH)
11.3 seconds (1958 Speedster model)

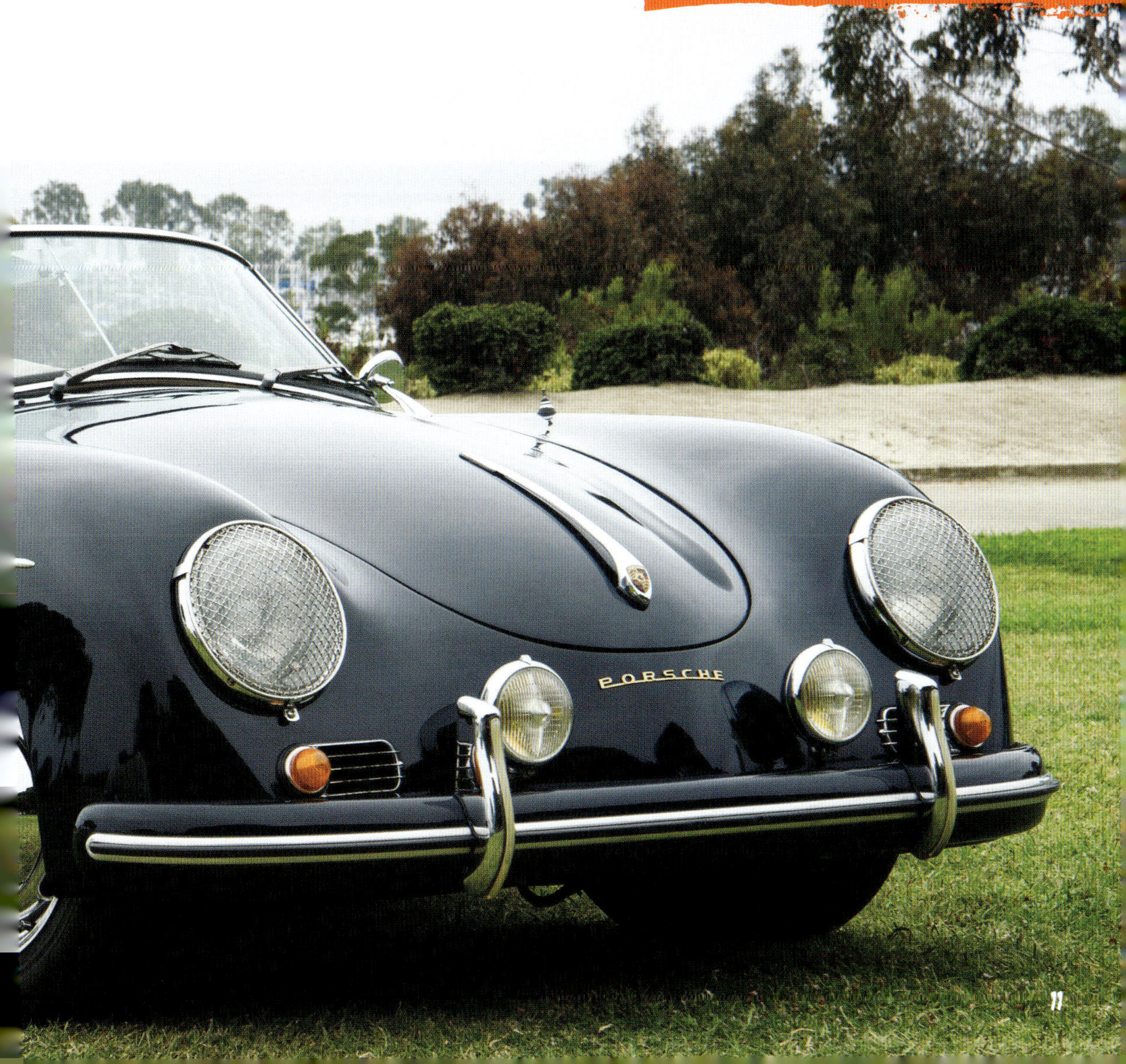

The Porsche 911 (nine-eleven) was introduced in 1963 as a larger and more powerful replacement for the 356. The 911's unique sloping roof made it one of the most popular sports car designs ever created. More than a million cars later, it is still in production.

PORSCHE 911
SPECIFICATIONS

YEARS PRODUCED
1964-Present

MAXIMUM HORSEPOWER
130 (1964 model)

ZERO TO 60 MPH (97 KPH)
8.3 seconds (1964 model)

XTREME FACT

The 911 was originally called the 901.
However, France's Peugeot car company
trademarked car models with 3 numbers
and a 0 in the middle. By 1964, Porsche's
new production models had the 911 name.

The 911 Carrera RS (racing sport) answered Porsche's wish to have a **production car** for **rally racing**. It was introduced in 1973. The thin-gauge steel metal body, thin glass, and plastic bumpers made it lightweight and fast. It had a 210 **horsepower** engine and a top speed of 149 mph (240 kph).

The 1973 Porsche 911 Carrera RS had a built-in "ducktail" spoiler.

XTREME FACT

In 1974, drivers Gijs van Lennep and Herbert Muller came in second in a Carrera RSR Turbo in the 24 Hours of Le Mans race.

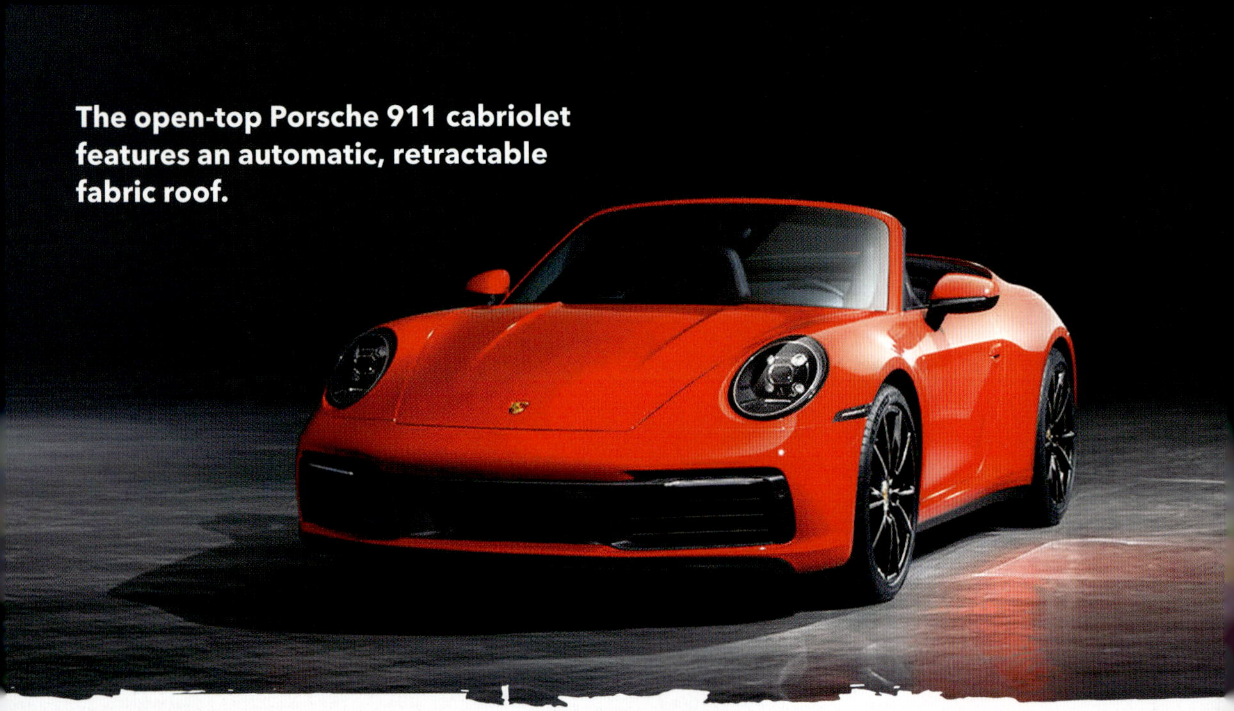

The open-top Porsche 911 cabriolet features an automatic, retractable fabric roof.

Today's Porsche 911 is available as a **cabriolet**, **coupe**, and **targa**. The modern 2-seater has a twin-turbo 6-cylinder engine that blasts the sports car

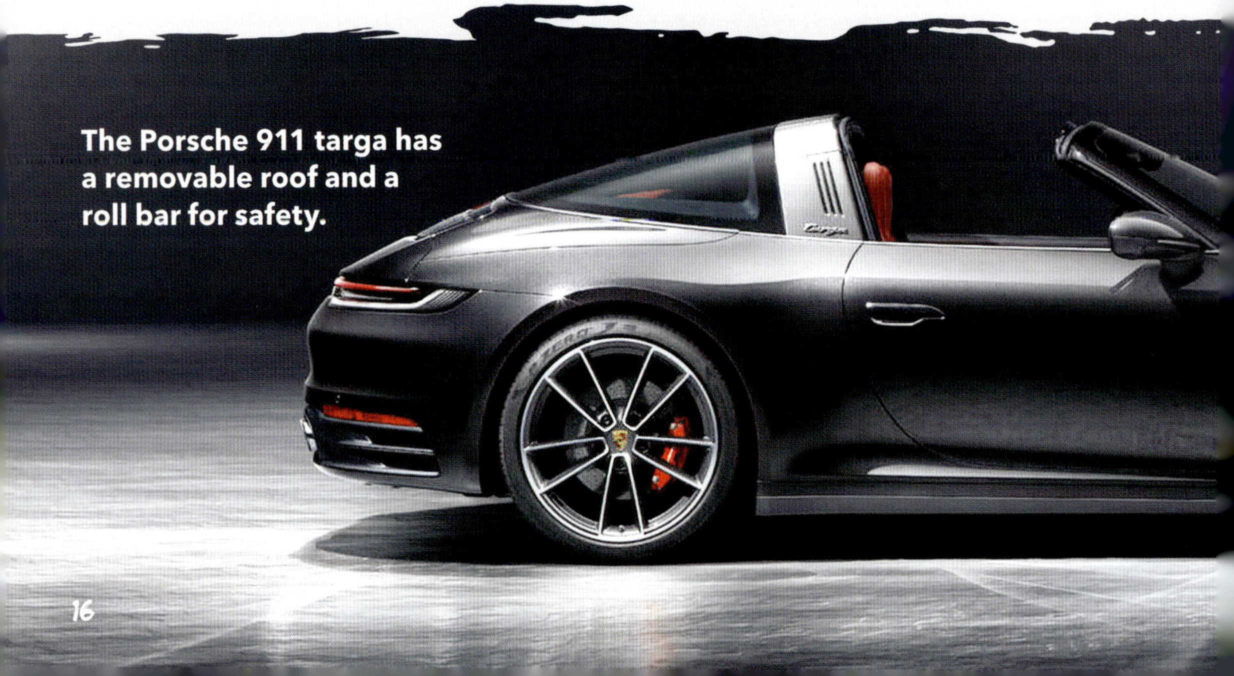

The Porsche 911 targa has a removable roof and a roll bar for safety.

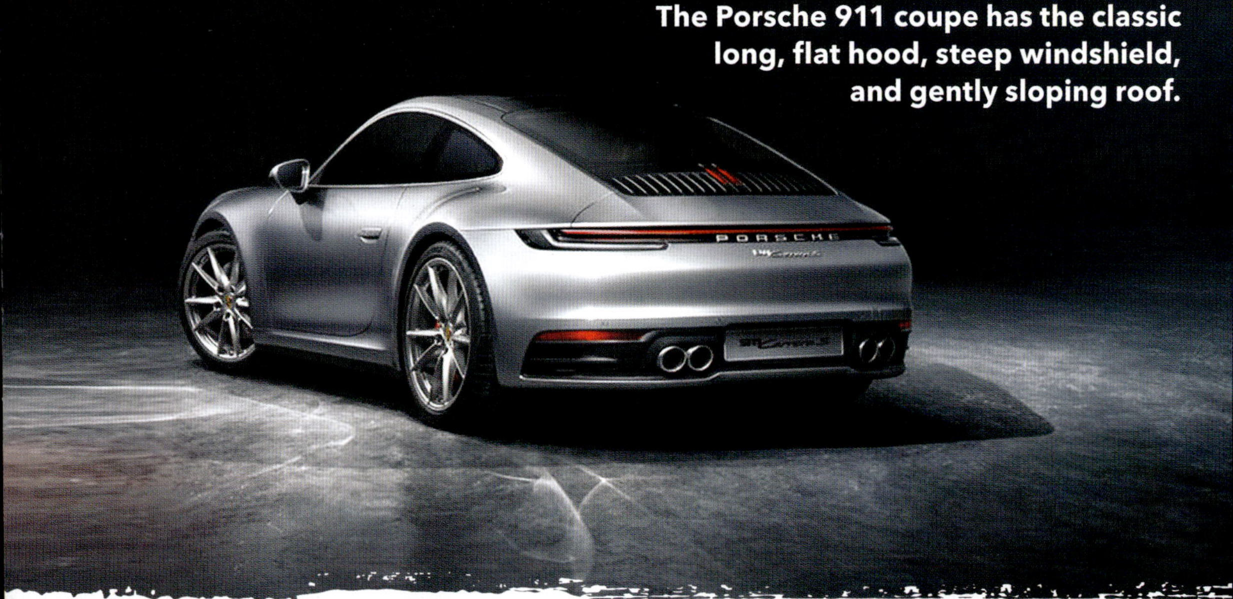

The Porsche 911 coupe has the classic long, flat hood, steep windshield, and gently sloping roof.

from 0-60 mph (97 kph) in 4.5 seconds. Designers mounted the engine in the center back of the car for greater stability and fewer vibrations at high speeds.

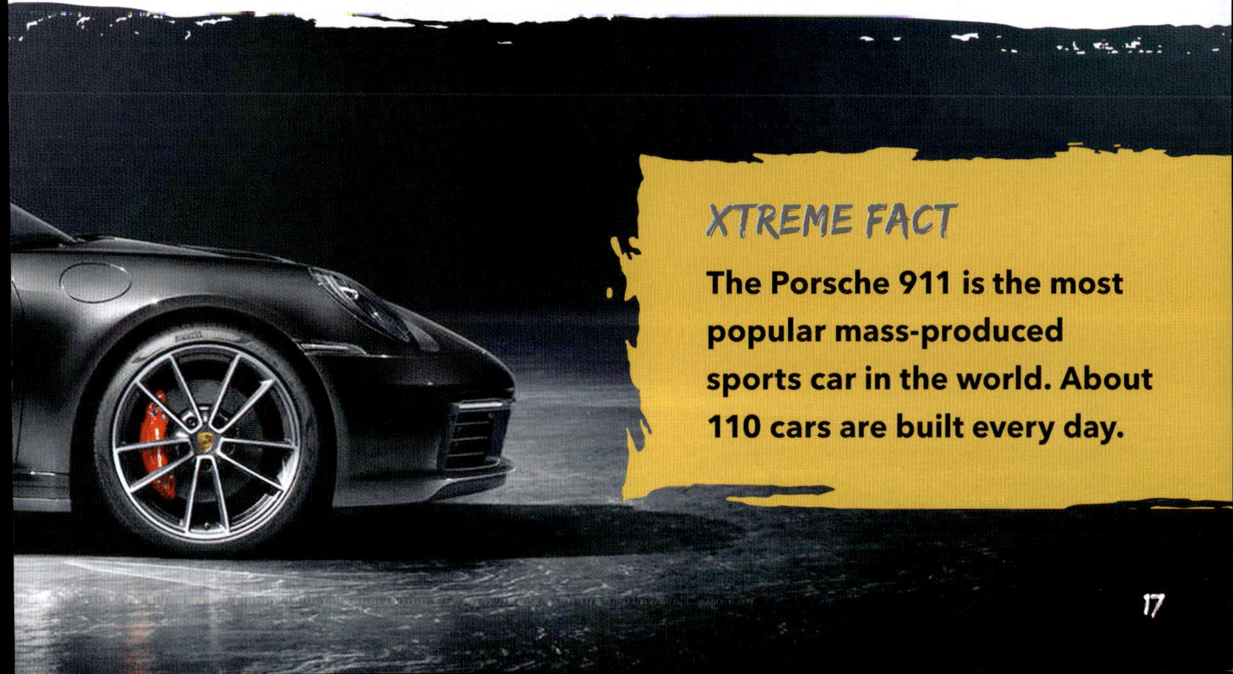

XTREME FACT

The Porsche 911 is the most popular mass-produced sports car in the world. About 110 cars are built every day.

CHAPTER 5

PORSCHE 928

The Porsche 928 was introduced in 1978. The **luxury grand tourer** was a 2+2 (two people in front and two people in back) design. A V8 engine powered the car to a top speed of 171 mph (275 kph). The 928's rounded **fastback** style gave it the nickname "The Egg."

YEARS PRODUCED
1978-1995

MAXIMUM HORSEPOWER
230 (1978 model)

ZERO TO 60 MPH (97 KPH)
6.3 seconds (1978 model)

The Porsche 928 was one of the first vehicles to have its bumpers built into the car's design. This created a flying saucer-like profile.

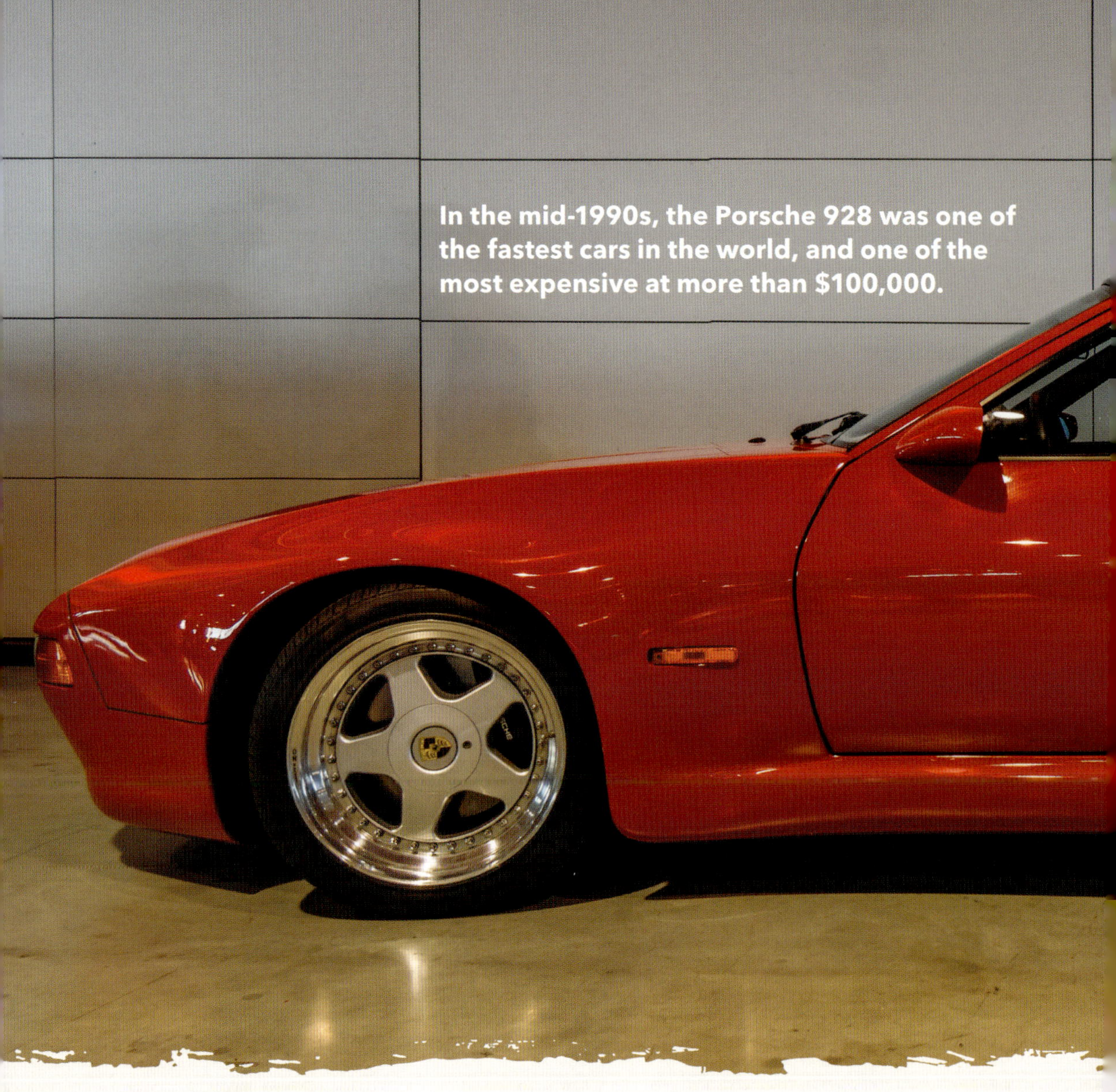

In 1978, a rear spoiler was added to the Porsche 928 to improve the car's **aerodynamics**. Car designer Vittorio Strosek gave the **grand tourer** a sleeker design in 1984. In 1995, the Porsche 928 had a 345 **horsepower** V8 engine. It reached a top speed of 171 mph (275 kph).

One of the Porsche 928's most famous features was the sports car's pop-up headlights.

CHAPTER 6

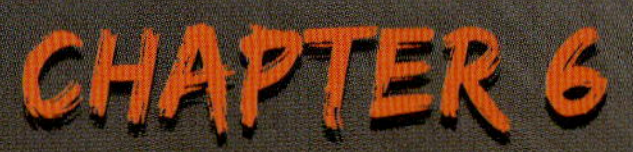

PORSCHE 944

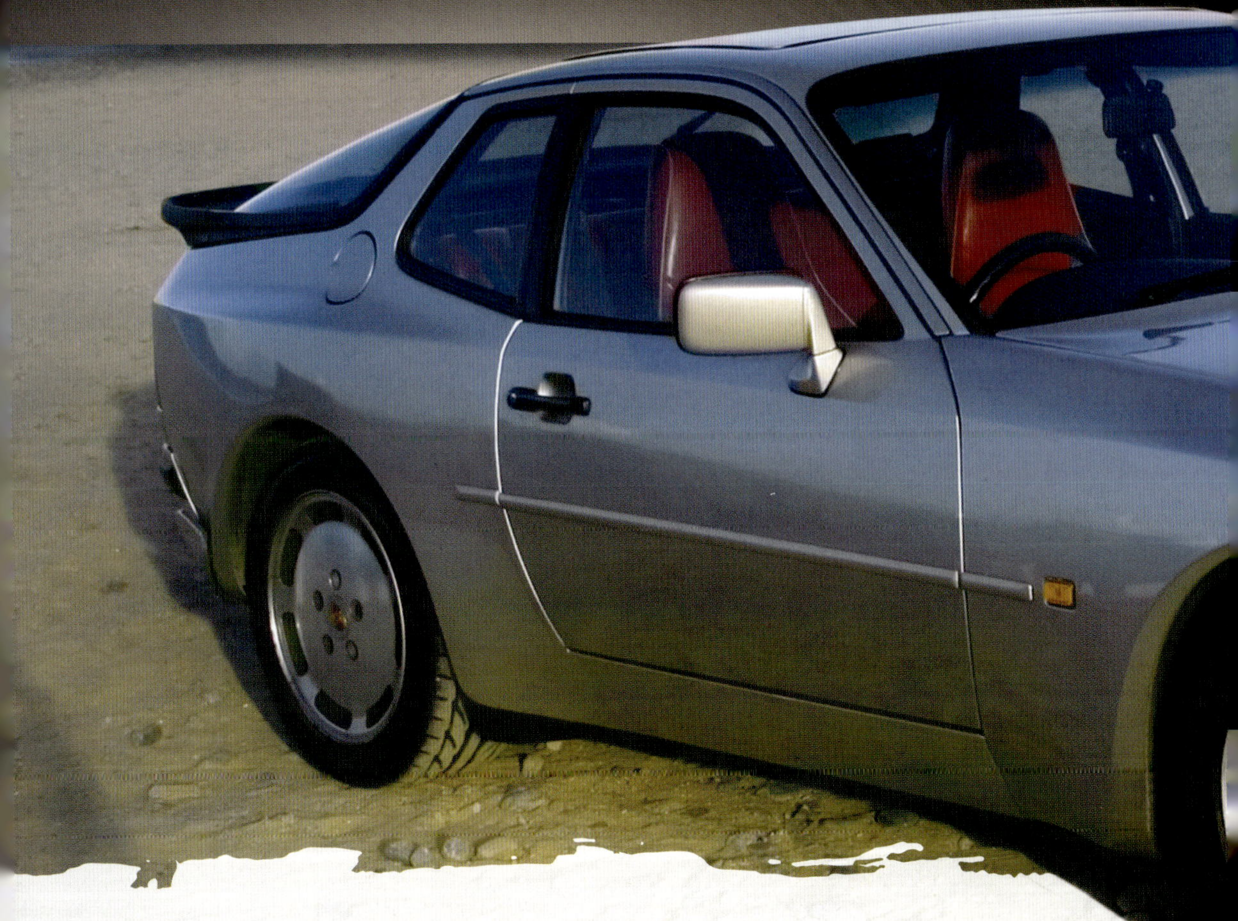

The Porsche 944 was introduced in 1982. It was a race car redesigned as a **grand tourer**. The 944 had a front engine that brought it to a top speed of 144 mph (232 kph).

The Porsche 944 had covered, pop-up headlights
and bumpers built into the car's design.

The Porsche 944 cabriolet had
a fabric top that was put up
and taken down by hand.

The 944 was available as a **coupe** and **cabriolet**. A turbo version was introduced in 1985. The turbo engine's 220 **horsepower** brought the car to a top speed of 152 mph (245 kph).

CHAPTER 7

PORSCHE BOXSTER & CAYMAN

The Porsche 986 came out in 1996 as a 2-seater **roadster** called the Boxster. As a mid-engine sports car, it had superior road handling and excellent performance. Its top speed was 149 mph (240 kph). The Boxster was only available as a **cabriolet**. Porsche introduced the **fastback coupe** version in 2005 as the Porsche 718 Cayman.

Porsche Boxster

Porsche Cayman

XTREME FACT

The name "Cayman" is an alternate spelling of caiman, a member of the alligator family. The hardtop car was a snappy version of its cousin, the Boxster.

The modern Boxster and Cayman came out in 2016, both with model number 718. Now a fourth generation, the redesigned 718s feature a new turbo engine. The Boxster and Cayman have a top speed of 170 mph (274 kph). The sports cars continue to be well known for their incredible road handling.

Porsche 718 Cayman

XTREME FACT

Nearly every Porsche vehicle has been made in Germany. However, from September 1997 to May 2011, the Boxster and Cayman were built in Finland by a company called Valmet. Assembly of the cars then returned to Germany.

Porsche 718 Boxster

CHAPTER 8

PORSCHE CARRERA GT

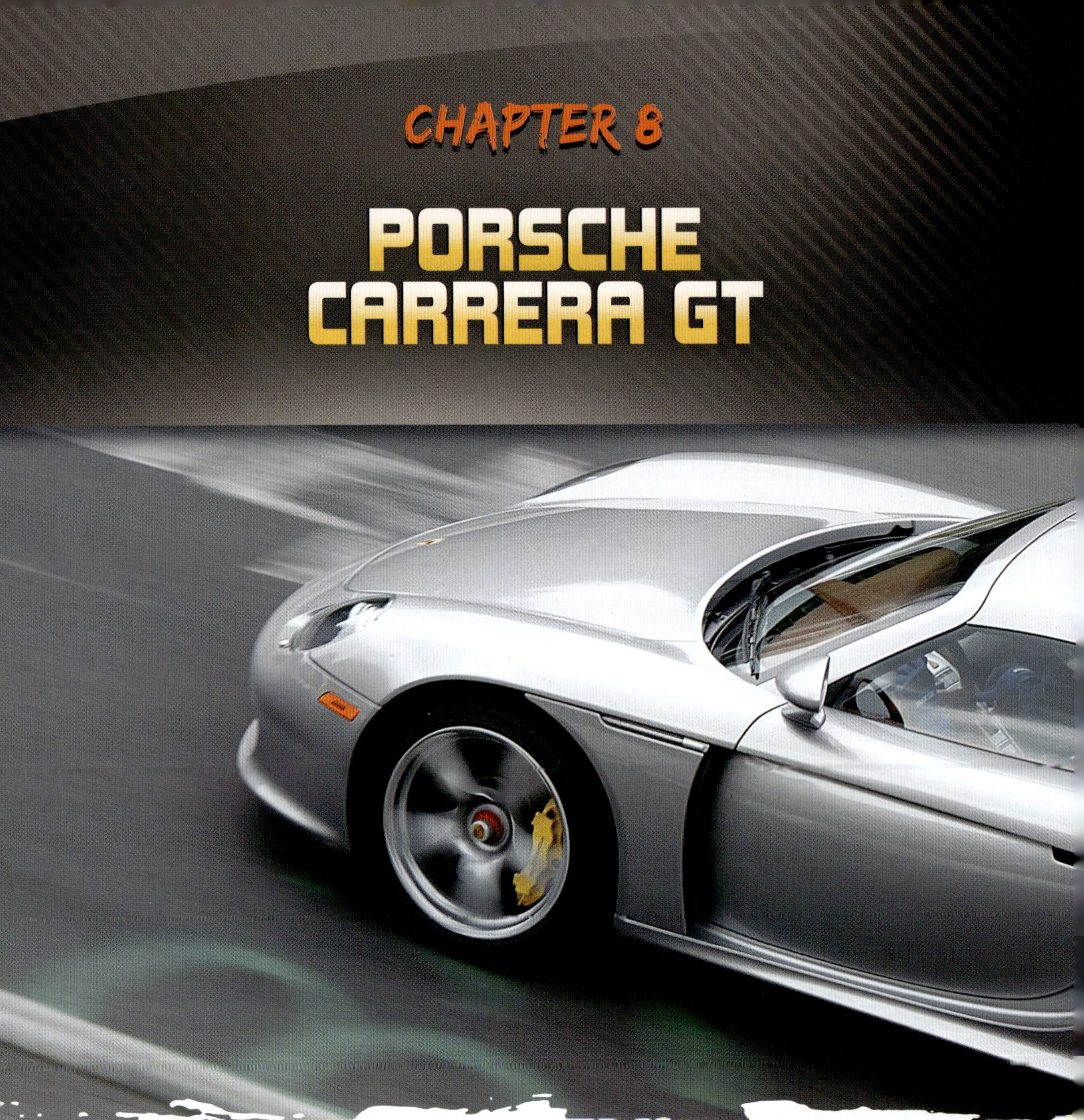

Model 980, the Porsche Carrera GT was Porsche's first **production car** made out of **carbon fiber**. Large side inlets and **air dams** helped cool the sports car's powerful V10 engine. With its lightweight body and powerful engine, it had a top speed of 205 mph (330 kph).

CARRERA GT
SPECIFICATIONS
YEARS PRODUCED
2003-2007
MAXIMUM HORSEPOWER
612 (2003 model)
ZERO TO 60 MPH (97 KPH)
3.4 seconds (2003 model)
Stainless steel sheets cover
the Carrera GT's engine, while
the rest of the body is carbon fiber.

The Porsche Carrera GT's low seats and balanced pedals gave it a racing car feel.

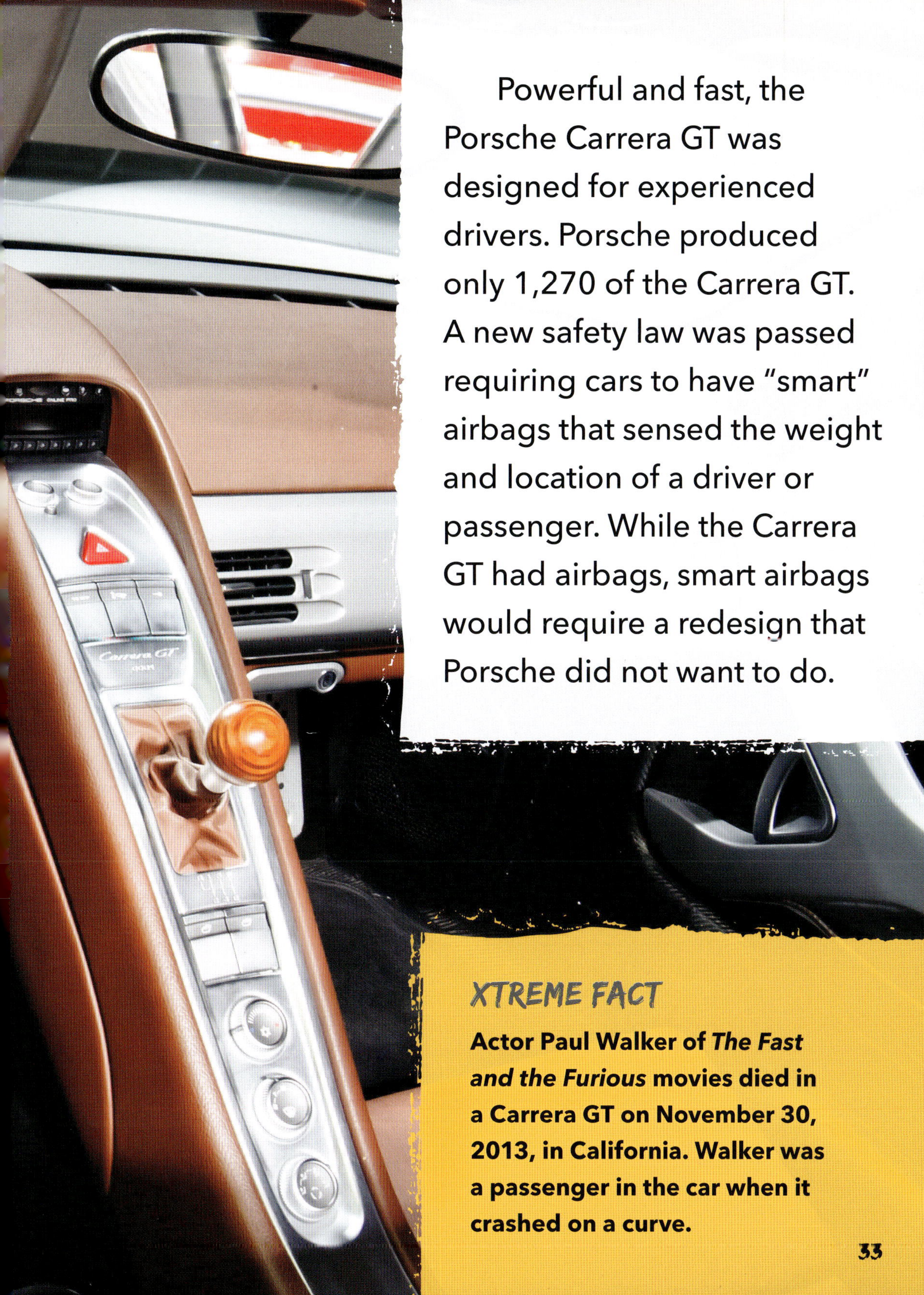

Powerful and fast, the Porsche Carrera GT was designed for experienced drivers. Porsche produced only 1,270 of the Carrera GT. A new safety law was passed requiring cars to have "smart" airbags that sensed the weight and location of a driver or passenger. While the Carrera GT had airbags, smart airbags would require a redesign that Porsche did not want to do.

XTREME FACT

Actor Paul Walker of *The Fast and the Furious* movies died in a Carrera GT on November 30, 2013, in California. Walker was a passenger in the car when it crashed on a curve.

CHAPTER 9

PORSCHE HYBRIDS

The 918 Spyder was Porsche's plug-in hybrid sports car first shown in 2010. With a top speed of 214 mph (344 kph), the 918 was a faster and more eco-friendly replacement for the Carrera GT.

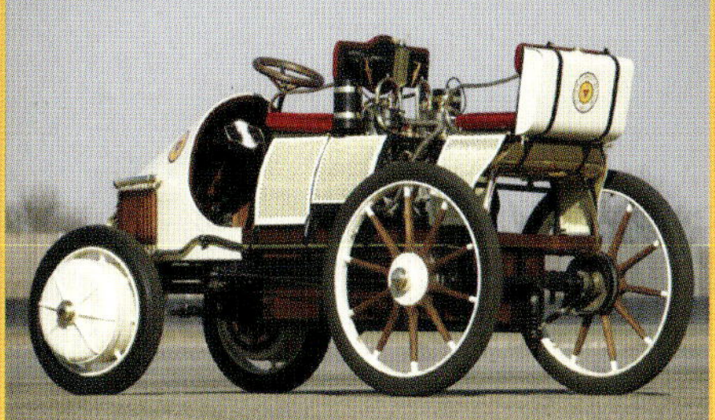

XTREME FACT

Ferdinand Porsche Sr. developed Porsche's first gas-electric hybrid vehicle in 1900. It was called Semper Vivus ("Always Alive").

918 SPYDER SPECIFICATIONS

YEARS PRODUCED
2013-2015

MAXIMUM HORSEPOWER
887 (2015 model)

ZERO TO 60 MPH (97 KPH)
2.2 seconds (2015 model)

A driver could flip a switch and turn off the 918's electric mode, allowing the battery to recharge with just a few minutes of gas-powered driving.

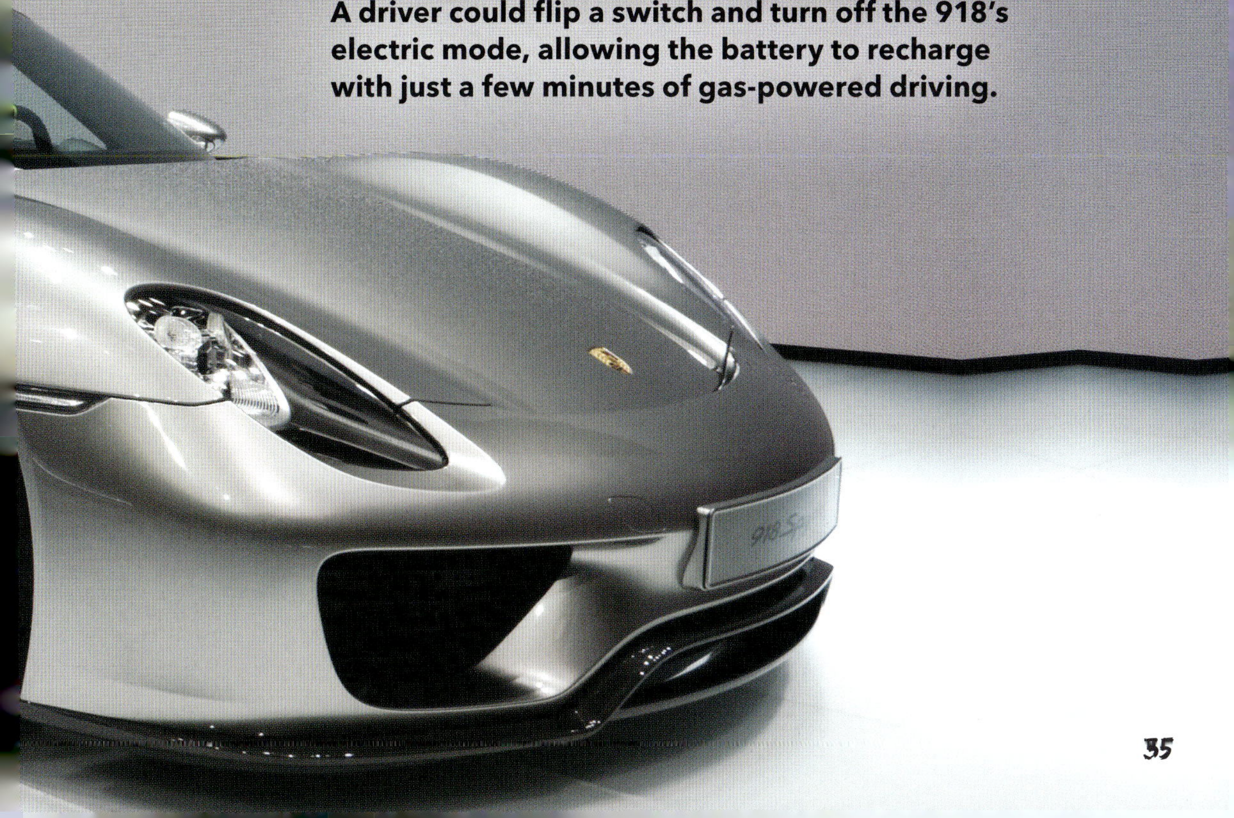

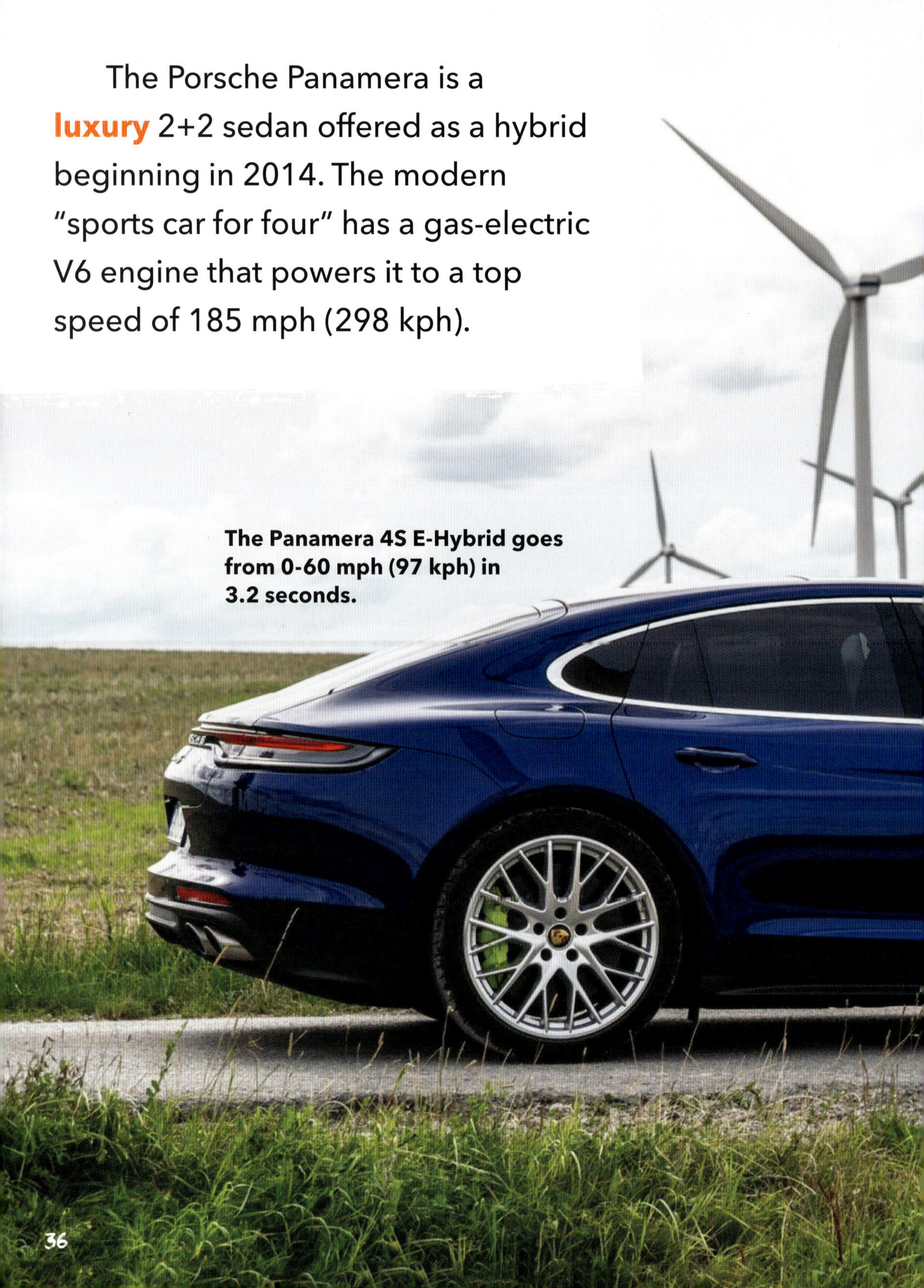

The Porsche Panamera is a **luxury** 2+2 sedan offered as a hybrid beginning in 2014. The modern "sports car for four" has a gas-electric V6 engine that powers it to a top speed of 185 mph (298 kph).

The Panamera 4S E-Hybrid goes from 0-60 mph (97 kph) in 3.2 seconds.

Porsche's Taycan Turbo hybrid is a super sports car introduced in 2019. Its two engines have 750 **horsepower**. The Taycan goes from 0-60 mph (97 kph) in 2.6 seconds. It has a top speed of 161 mph (259 kph).

XTREME FACT

Porsche's Taycan has a Launch Control function that gives maximum acceleration from a standing start. In the first 2.5 seconds, the Taycan Turbo S covers more ground than a 918 Spyder.

PORSCHE RACE CARS

Porsches have been winners in **production car** and **rally races** for decades. A Porsche 911 won the Monte Carlo Rally in 1968, 1969, and 1970. Porsche 917, 935, and 936 were popular cars in the 24 Hours of Le Mans **endurance race**, with a 917K winning in 1970 and 1971.

In 1970, Björn Waldegård and Lars Helmer race to win the Monte Carlo Rally in a Porsche 911S.

In 1970, drivers Hans Herrmann and Richard Attwood won the 24 Hours of Le Mans in a Porsche 917K.

Porsche continues to compete in modern **endurance races**. A Porsche V8 won the 2010 Rolex 24 at Daytona International Speedway in Florida. The dependability, power, and speed of a Porsche brings racing wins.

After 24 hours of racing, Mike Rockenfeller, Ryan Dalziel, João Barbosa, and Terry Borcheller win in a Porsche V8 at the 2010 Rolex 24 at Daytona race.

FELLER ▶ R.DALZIEL
T. BORCHELLER
Porsche V8
BY LBP
PIRELLI
ROLEX 24
mimi so
PENSKE
BOSCH
AP
EMCO
ayton
MoTeC
Airpas
WILSON MANIFOLDS

CHAPTER 11

THE FUTURE

Porsche's future will see more hybrid cars. The company is also experimenting with a synthetic fuel called eFuel. It burns the same as regular gasoline, but is much cleaner. Since 70 percent of Porsche cars are still running, drivers may have an environmentally friendly fuel for their beloved Porsche cars.

A Porsche 718 Cayman GT4 RS runs on eFuel.

XTREME CHALLENGE

**TAKE THE QUIZ BELOW AND
PUT WHAT YOU'VE LEARNED TO THE TEST!**

1) The Porsche logo is a tribute to what city and country? Does the company still operate there?

2) Who said, "I looked around and could not find quite the car I dreamed of, so I decided to build it myself"?

3) What was Porsche's first production car model?

4) Porsche 911s come in three different roof styles. What are they?

5) What Porsche grand tourer was nicknamed "The Egg?" Why was it called that?

6) What was Porsche's first production car to be made out of carbon fiber? What is its top speed?

7) Name three Porsche hybrid cars.

8) What is the name of Porsche's cleaner, synthetic fuel?

GLOSSARY

aerodynamic – Something that has a shape that reduces the drag, or resistance, of air moving across its surface. Cars with aerodynamic shapes can go faster because they don't have to push as hard to get through the air.

air dam – A device on the front of a sports or race car that helps steady the vehicle while channeling cool air to the engine.

cabriolet – Another word for convertible. A car with a roof that retracts or folds down.

carbon fiber – A very strong, thin, and lightweight fiber made of carbon atoms. It may be used in the bodies of cars, planes, and boats.

coupe – A passenger car with a fixed roof that cannot be removed, usually with two or three doors. Coupes have a sportier look than four-door sedans, with a sloping rear roofline.

endurance race – An auto race that requires drivers and their cars to handle many hours of near-constant driving.

fastback – A car with a roof that has a long curving downward slope to the back of the vehicle.

grand tourer (GT) – Cars that can be driven on public roads. GT cars are designed for both performance and comfort.

horsepower (HP) – A unit of measure of power. The term was originally invented to compare the power output by a steam engine with that of an average draft horse.

luxury – Something that adds pleasure or comfort, and is often expensive.

production car – A model of car that is produced by a company that all look the same and are sold to the public.

rally race – A race that takes place on public or private roads with modified production or specially built road-legal cars.

roadster – A car with an open roof that seats two people.

targa – A removable, hard roof on a car. It allows the vehicle to become a convertible or open-top.

ONLINE RESOURCES

To learn more about Porsche, please visit abdobooklinks.com or scan this QR code. These links are routinely monitored and updated to provide the most current information available.

INDEX